Hand book of Systematic Bacteriology:

Basic Staining and Biochemical Techniques

Kaustubh Mani

About the Author

Kaustubh Mani is a dedicated and talented undergraduate student pursuing a Bachelor's degree in Medical Laboratory Science at Jeevan Jyoti Institute of Nursing and Paramedical Sciences, Aligarh, Uttar Pradesh (affiliated with Atal Bihari Vajpayee Medical University,U.P. Lucknow). His area of interest lies in Microbiology, and he is deeply engaged in his studies in this field.

Apart from academics, Kaustubh is a freelance journalist, contributing to various Hindi media platforms. He is also a passionate social worker, particularly in animal welfare, collaborating with several NGOs to make a positive impact.

Through this book, Kaustubh aims to share his knowledge and insights with readers.

Introduction

The field of bacteriology has long been a cornerstone of microbiological research and diagnostics, with staining and biochemical examination techniques playing a crucial role in the identification and characterization of bacteria. These techniques, honed over decades, form the bedrock of laboratory practices, enabling scientists and healthcare professionals to understand bacterial morphology, physiology, and pathogenicity.

This book aims to provide a comprehensive guide to the techniques and procedures involved in staining and biochemical examination in bacteriology. From the foundational Gram stain to advanced biochemical tests, this book covers the essential methods used in the laboratory to identify and classify bacteria. Each chapter is designed to offer detailed protocols, practical tips, and insights into the interpretation of results, making it an invaluable resource for students, researchers, and clinical microbiologists alike.

Whether you are a novice in the field or an experienced professional, this book seeks to enhance your understanding and proficiency in these fundamental techniques. By bridging the gap between theory and practice, it aims to support the next generation of microbiologists in their pursuit of knowledge and innovation.

Through this work, we hope to contribute to the advancement of bacteriological research and diagnostics, ultimately improving our ability to combat bacterial infections and promote public health.

Table of Contents

➢ ***Bacterial Culture & Staining Techniques***

➢ ***Biochemical Tests for Identification of Bacteria***

Bacterial Culture & Staining Techniques

Seed Culture

A small, precultured bacterial sample that contains actively dividing cells.

Purpose:

To ensure rapid and healthy growth in the main culture.

Procedure:

1. Inoculation:
   A single colony from the growth culture is transferred into a small volume of liquid medium (broth).
2. Incubation:
   Incubate at 37 °C to grow a dense, healthy culture.
3. Transfer:
   A measured volume of the prepared seed culture is then added to a large volume of fresh medium to start the main culture.

Applications:

- Protein expression
- Antibiotic production
- Fermentation processes.

Staining techniques

Staining

A technique used to enhance and contrast a biological specimen under a microscope by applying dyes.

Simple Staining

In this method, only one stain is used, and all bacteria are stained similarly.

This technique is mainly used to identify the shape, size, and arrangement of bacteria.

Commonly Used Stains:

- Loeffler's Methylene Blue (gives blue-colored colonies)
- Dilute Carbol Fuchsin (gives pink-colored colonies)

Principle:

Simple staining is based on the interaction between the dye's positively charged chromophore and the negatively charged components of the bacterial cell.

Requirements:

- Inoculating loop
- Distilled water
- Spirit lamp
- Microscopic glass slide

- Blotting paper
- Stain (Loeffler's Methylene Blue or Dilute Carbol Fuchsin)
- Bacterial culture plate

Procedure:

1. Disinfect the table surface.
2. Flame the inoculating loop over the spirit lamp until red-hot, then allow it to cool.
3. Take a glass slide and place a drop of distilled water in the middle using the inoculating loop.
4. Take a small portion of a bacterial colony from the agar plate and emulsify it with the drop of water on the slide.
5. Spread the smear to about 1 cm^2 to form a thin film.
6. Allow the slide to air dry for 2 to 3 minutes.
7. After air drying, fix the smear by passing the slide quickly over the flame (heat fixation).
8. Place the fixed smear over the staining rack.
9. Add stain over the smear and let it stand for 3 to 4 minutes.
10. Wash the slide gently with distilled water.
11. Blot dry the smear using blotting paper.
12. Now the stained smear is ready for microscopic examination.

13. Observe the slide under the microscope using a 100X oil immersion objective.

Observation:

The color of the organism depends on the stain used:

- Loeffler's Methylene Blue → Blue-colored colonies
- Dilute Carbol Fuchsin → Pink-colored colonies

Dyes Used in Simple Staining:

- Basic Dyes:
    - Positively charged
    - Bind to negatively charged molecules like nucleic acids and proteins.
- Acidic Dyes:
    - Negatively charged
    - Bind to positively charged cell structures.
    - They stain best under acidic conditions when proteins and other molecules carry a positive charge.

Gram Staining

It is a differential staining technique used to differentiate bacteria into gram positive and gram negative type according to their cell wall structure.

Principle:

The gram stain differentiates between gram positive and gram negative bacteria based on their cell wall structures, espically the thickness of peptidoglycan layer and presence of an outer membrane.

Requirements:

- Crystal Violet (Primary Stain)
- Gram's iodine (Mordant)
- 95% Ethyl alcohol (Decolorizer)
- Safranin (Counter stain)

Procedure:

1. Take a clean glass slide.

2. Put 2–3 drops of distilled water on the slide using a dropper.

3. Inoculate a small amount of bacterial colony with an inoculating loop.

4. Mix the sample with the distilled water on the slide and spread it to form a thin smear.

5. Allow the smear to air dry.

6. Heat-fix the smear by passing the slide through a flame gently.

7. Flood the smear with crystal violet stain and leave for 1 minute.

8. Wash the slide gently under running tap water.

9. Apply Gram's iodine solution and leave for 1 minute.

10. Wash the slide again under running tap water.

11. Decolorize the smear by adding a few drops of 95% ethyl alcohol for 10–15 seconds.

12. Immediately wash the slide with running tap water.

13. Counterstain the smear by adding a few drops of safranin and leave for 1 minute.

14. Wash the slide gently under running tap water.

15. Allow the slide to air dry by placing it on a slide rack.

16. Observe the slide under a microscope under oil immersion.

Observation:

- Gram-positive bacteria appear purple/violet.
- Gram-negative bacteria appear pink/red.

Ziehl-Neelsen Staining

Principle:

Ziehl-Neelsen stain (Acid Fast stain) is used for staining Mycobacteria, which are hardly stained by Gram's staining method. Once the mycobacteria is stained, it cannot be decolorized by acid. It is also known as acid-fast bacteria.

Requirements:

- Carbol Fuchsin
- Acid Alcohol
- Methylene Blue / Malachite Green

Procedure:

1. Prepare the smear from the primary specimen and fix it by passing through the flame and label clearly.

2. Place fixed slide on staining rack and cover each slide with carbol fuchsin solution.

3. Heat the slide on spirit lamp until vapour rises and wait for 3 to 5 minutes.

4. Wash the stain with clean water.

5. Decolorize the smear with 3% acid alcohol until all colour is removed (two minutes).

6. Counterstain the slide with 0.1% methylene blue for one minute.

7. Wash off the stain with clean water and air dry it.

8. Examine the smear under oil immersion (100x objective).

Observation:

- Acid-fast bacilli → *Red colour*
- Background → Blue colour

Spore Staining

Spore Staining is also known as 'Endospore Staining'

Principle:

Unlike most vegetative cell types that stain by common procedures, the free spore, because of its impervious coats, will not accept the primary stain easily. For further penetration, the application of heat is required.

After the primary stain is applied and the smear is heated, both the vegetative cell and spore will appear green.

Requirements:

1. Decolorizing Agent:

Once the spore accepts the malachite green, it cannot be decolorized by tap water, which removes only the excess primary stain. The spore remains green.

The stain does not demonstrate a strong affinity for vegetative cell components i.e., the water removes it and the cells will appear colorless.

2. Counterstain (Safranin):

In contrast, red stain is used as second reagent to colour the decolorized vegetative cells which will absorb the counterstain and appear red. The spores retain green of primary stain.

Procedure:

1. Prepare a smear of the spore-forming bacteria and fix in flame.

2. Cover the smear with 5% malachite green solution and heat over steaming water bath for 2–3 min.

3. Wash with clean water.

4. Apply 1% safranin for 30 seconds.

5. Wash with clean water.

6. Dry and examine under oil immersion objective.

Observations:

1. Endospore – Bright green

2. Vegetative cells – Brownish red to pink

Capsule Staining

Principle:

This technique is used to detect capsules around bacterial cells. The capsule is a gelatinous layer composed mainly of polysaccharides or polypeptides. It does not readily absorb stains. This technique uses a combination of acidic and basic stains to highlight both the bacterial cell and capsule. The capsule remains unstained, creating a clear halo around the bacterial cell.

Procedure:

1.Preparation of Smear: A bacterial sample is placed on a clean glass slide, and mixed with a drop of India ink or nigrosin (acidic stain).

2.Spread the Sample:Use another slide to spread the sample evenly and form a thin smear.

3.Air Dry: Allow the slide to air dry; do not heat-fix, as it will distort the capsules.

4.Staining: Stain the slide with a basic stain such as crystal violet for about 1 minute.

5.Rinse Gently: Gently rinse the slide with distilled water to remove excess stain.

6. Air Dry: Allow the slide to air dry again.

7.Observe:Observe the slide under a microscope.

Observations:

The capsule will appear as a clear, colorless halo surrounding the bacterial cell. The bacterial cell will appear stained with the basic dye (purple in crystal violet). The background will be darkened by the acidic stain (black in India ink or nigrosin).

Negative Staining

Principle:

Acid dyes have a negative charge. These stains are repelled by the negatively charged bacterial cell. As a result, the specimen remains clear or transparent against a stained or dark background.

Requirements:

1. Nigrosin: A common dye used for negative staining, which stains the background and leaves the cells or structures of interest unstained.

2. India ink: Another commonly used reagent for negative staining, particularly for visualizing capsules or slime layers around bacteria.

Procedure:

1. Place a drop of the specimen on one end of a clean slide.
2. Add a small drop of nigrosin (or India ink) to the bacterial suspension.
3. Using the edge of another slide, spread the mixture across the first slide to create a thin smear.
4. Allow the smear to air dry completely.
5. Observe the slide under a microscope

Types of Negative Staining:

1. Spore/Endospore staining
2. Capsule staining
3. Simple negative staining

Advantages:

- Clear, unstained cell can be easily observed against a dark or black stained background.
- It can stain heat-sensitive cells.

Disadvantages:

- Can only give information about the shape and size of bacteria.

Albert Staining

Principle:

Albert stain is basically made up of two stains that are toluidine blue O and malachite green. Both solutions are basic dyes with high affinity for acidic tissue components like cytoplasm.The pH range of Albert stain is adjusted to 2.8 by using acetic acid, which becomes basic for volutin granules as the pH of volutin granules is slightly acidic.

Therefore, on applying Albert stain to the smear, toluidine blue O stains volutin granules reddish-purple. It is the most acidic part of the cell and malachite green stains the cytoplasm blue-green. On adding iodine, due to the effect of iodine, the metachromatic property is not observed, and granules appear blue in colour.

Requirements:

1. Albert Stain I

Toluidine blue 0.15g

Malachite green 0.20g

Glacial acetic acid 1.0ml

Alcohol (95%) 2.0ml

Distilled water 100ml

2. Albert Stain II (Iodine)

Iodine 2.0g

Potassium iodide 3.0g

Distilled water 300ml

Procedure:

1. Take a clean slide.
2. Prepare a smear on a clean slide.
3. Air dry and heat-fix the smear.
4. Treat the smear with Albert stain I and allow it to react for 3 minutes.
5. Drain the excess stain; do not wash.
6. Flood the smear with Albert stain II (Iodine) for 2 minutes.
7. Wash the slide with distilled water and air dry it.
8. Observe the slide under oil immersion microscope.

Observations:

The metachromatic granules will appear bluish-black, whereas the body of the bacilli appears light green.

Nesser Staining

Principle:

It is a test for the presence of polyphosphate stored in the cells. This method is indispensable and aids in the identification of certain strains of Corynebacterium bacteria. Further, this staining method can make the "beaded" bacteria responsible for biological phosphate removal visible.

Requirements:

(A)

Methylene blue 0.1g

Glacial acetic acid 5ml

Ethanol 96% 5ml

Distilled water 100ml

(B)

Crystal violet, 10% in 96% ethanol 3.3ml

Ethanol 96% 6.7ml

Distilled water 100ml

(C)

Chrysoidin Y, 1% aq. solution 33.3ml

Distilled water 100ml

Procedure:

1)Prepare a fixed smear.

2)Place a freshly made mixture of 2 parts solution A and 1 part solution B onto the smear for a contact period of 10-15 seconds. Allow excess solution to run off the slide.

3)Add solution C for a contact period of 45 seconds.

4) Rinse the slide with tap water.

5)Allow the slide to air dry and view under the 100x bright field objective. Granules can be spotted as highly refractile and most often located at the poles.

Observation:

- Corynebacterium bacteria will stain completely light brown.
- Volutin granules will stain dark purple or bluish-black.

Wet mount Staining

Principle:

The Flagella staining uses a mordant to thicken the bacterial flagella that are too thin to be stained.

Requirement:

Solution - I (Mordant)

(1) 5% aq. solution of phenol: 10ml

(2) Tannic acid: 2g

(3) Aluminum potassium sulfate: 10ml

Solution - II

(1) Crystal violet: 12g

(2) 95% Ethanol

(Combinedly are called Ryu stain)

Procedure:

1. Clean the Slide and Coverslip:* Ensure both are clean and grease-free.
2. Prepare the Sample:

Liquid Culture: Place a small drop of the bacterial suspension onto the center of a clean microscope slide. Be careful not to use too much liquid, as it will make it difficult to focus.

Solid Culture:Gently touch a sterile loop to a colony and then emulsify the bacteria in a small drop of sterile broth or distilled water on the slide. Avoid creating a dense suspension.

3. Apply the Coverslip: Carefully lower a clean coverslip onto the drop at a slight angle to avoid trapping air bubbles.

4. Observe Under the Microscope:

1)Place the slide on the microscope stage.

2)Start with a low power objective (10x) to locate the bacteria.

3)Switch to a higher power objective (40x) to observe individual cells.

To observe motility:Look for movement of the bacteria across the field of view. True motility is directional and independent, unlike Brownian motion (random jiggling).To attempt to visualize flagella: This is the challenging part. You'll need high magnification (400x or 1000x with oil immersion) and careful focusing. The flagella, if visible, will appear as thin, thread-like appendages extending from the bacterial cells. The optional dilute stain might make them slightly more discernible. Reducing the light intensity can sometimes help in visualizing delicate structures.

6. Record Observations: Note whether motility is present and attempt to describe the number and arrangement of any visible flagella.

Results:

The flagella will stain purple.

Fontana Stain for Spirochetes

Principle:

The principle of the Fontana stain involves the use of a mordant (tannic acid and phenol) to thicken the delicate spirochetes, making them more visible. The silver nitrate solution then deposits metallic silver onto the spirochetes, staining them a dark brown or black color against a light background. The initial fixation step with formaldehyde preserves the morphology of the spirochetes and ensures their adherence to the slide.

Requirements:

1. Fontana's Fixative
2. Fontana's Stain
3. Fontana's Mordant
4. 95% Ethanol

5.Tartar sample

Procedure:

1. Take a clean slide; alcohol and flame sterilize the pin.

2. This sterilized pin is used to collect the serous tartar sample present in the deeper spaces of teeth.

3.Now, this tartar sample is mixed in the sterile distilled water, and the suspension stain is formed.

4. A drop of this suspension is taken with the help of a sterile wire loop on a clean grease-free slide, and a smear is prepared.

5. This smear is air-dried but not heat-fixed, as the cells are very sensitive.

6. This smear is fixed by using chemical fixative, i.e., Fontana's Fixative. Use 2-3 drops of Fontana's Fixative for 3 minutes at an interval of 1 minute.

7. After the fixative is washed off, the slide is treated with 95% alcohol for 3 minutes.

8. After 3 minutes, the excess alcohol is washed off, and the slide is flooded with the help of forceps and pipette through flame to remove excess alcohol.

9.Fontana's mordant is added on the smear and heated until steam appears.

10. After steam appears, the slide is washed with water and air-dried.

11.This slide is now treated with Fontana's stain and heated until steam rises.

12. After steam rises, the slide is washed with distilled water and air-dried.

13, Observe the slide under oil immersion.

Results:

The spirochetes are stained brownish-black in color.

Biochemical test for identification of bacteria

Catalase Test

Catalase is an enzyme produced by all living plants, animals, and some species of bacteria which are always exposed to O_2. These organisms are present in aerobic environments.

The bacteria that conduct aerobic metabolism produce H_2O_2 as toxic product of their metabolism. Toxic H_2O_2 can cause damage to DNA,protein,lipids.

The cell produce this enzyme to break down H_2O_2 into H_2O and O_2..This test is used to differentiate between bacteria that produce catalase enzyme and those that don't.

{Bacteria can only make catalase if they have the gene for catalase in their DNA.}

Principle:

Catalase mediates the breakdown of hydrogen peroxide into oxygen and water. To test if a particular bacterial isolate can produce catalase enzyme, a small inoculum of a bacterial isolate is mixed into 3% hydrogen peroxide solution. If observed, rapid elaboration of bubbles indicates the presence of catalase. The lack of catalase is evidenced by the lack of bubble formation.

- ***Test tube method***

The procedure is performed in a sterile test tube.

Requirements:

1. Bacterial culture

2. Sterile technique
3. Dropper
4. Wire loop
5. Hydrogen peroxide solution

Procedure:

1. Add 1-2 ml hydrogen peroxide solution into a test tube.

2. Using a sterile loop or nichrome wire, add a colony of the test culture to the hydrogen peroxide containing test tube.

Result:

- Immediate bubble formation **(catalase +ve).**
- No bubbles are observed. **(Catalase -ve)**

➢ ***Slide method***

This test is performed on a clean slide.

Requirements:

1. Bacterial culture
2. Clean glass-free slide
3. Wire loop
4. Hydrogen peroxide solution

Procedure:

1. Use a sterile loop to transfer a small amount of colony growth to the surface of a clean slide.

2. Place 2-3 drops of 3% hydrogen peroxide on the glass slide.

Result:

- Bubbles are observed. **(Catalase +ve, Bubbles)**
- No bubbles are observed. **(Catalase -ve, No bubbles)**

Coagulase Test

Coagulase enzyme is produced by Staphylococcus aureus. It can cause coagulation (clotting) of blood plasma.

Principle:

Some bacteria like Staphylococcus aureus produce an enzyme called coagulase.This enzyme is responsible for clotting plasma. There are two types of coagulase:

- Bound coagulase — reacts directly with plasma components and causes clumping of bacterial cells.
- Free coagulase— reacts with plasma factors and leads to clot formation.

When free coagulase reacts, it converts fibrinogen into fibrin, resulting in a solid clot.

➢ *Test tube method*

Requirements:

1. Citrated plasma (usually rabbit plasma)
2. Bacterial growth from any solid medium
3. 3 test tubes
4. Dropper or pipette
5. Inoculating loop

Procedure:

1. Take 3 test tubes and label them as '+ve' (positive control), '-ve' (negative control), and 'test'.
2. Prepare a dilution of plasma using Normal Saline (N.S.).
3. Add 2 full pipettes (about 2 ml) of the diluted plasma into each test tube.
4. Inoculate the test tube with your bacterial sample.

Note:

Incubate all tubes at 35°C.Check for clot formation after 1 hour, 2 hours, and 4 hours by gently tilting the tubes at 90°. If no clot is observed even after 4 hours, keep the tubes at room temperature for 10–18 hours and recheck.

Result:

- **Positive Test:**Clot formation (the plasma solidifies).
- **Negative Test:** No clot formation (the plasma remains liquid)

➤ ***Slide Method***

Requirements:

1. 3 slides
2. Normal saline (N.S.)
3. Plasma
4. Bacterial colony from solidified medium
5. Inoculating loop

Procedure:

1. Place a drop of N.S. on each of the 3 slides.

2. Pick a bacterial colony using the inoculating loop and emulsify it properly into the saline drop until it becomes milky.

3. Add a small drop of plasma beside the emulsified colony and mix gently.

Result:

- **Positive test:** Formation of visible clumps.
- **Negative test:** No clumping is seen.

Indole Test

The Indole Test is used to check if a bacterium can produce specific enzymes that break down the amino acid tryptophan into indole. If the organism has these enzymes, it will produce indole when grown in a medium containing tryptophan. This indole can be detected using a reagent called Kovac's reagent, which reacts with indole to form a red or pink-colored layer at the top of the broth.

Principle:

Some bacteria can chop up the amino acid tryptophan and release a substance called indole. When we add a special chemical (Kovac's reagent), if indole is there, it reacts and makes a red colour appear. That's how we know the bacteria can break down tryptophan.

Requirements:

1. Broth

2. Bacterial sample

3. Broth containing tryptophan or sulphide indole motility medium

4. Inoculation loop

5. Kovac's reagent

Procedure:

1. Add bacterial culture into broth containing tryptophan.

2. Inoculate the broth using the help of an inoculating loop.
3. Incubate at 37°C for 24 hours.
4. Add Kovac's reagent to the top of the broth.

Result:

- **A positive test** will show a red colour on the surface of the broth.
- **A negative test :**no change (remains yellow).

Note:

After incubation, Kovac's reagent is added to the test tube by dropping it gently onto the agar surface. Kovac's reagent typically contains p-dimethylaminobenzaldehyde, which reacts with indole to produce a red or pink colour.

Methyl Red Test

The Methyl Red (MR) test is used to check if the bacteria can produce a lot of strong acids (like lactic acid, acetic acid) by breaking down glucose.

Principle:

Some bacteria break down glucose and make strong acids. These acids lower the pH of the solution. Methyl Red is a chemical that changes colour if the pH gets very low. If the bacteria produce enough acid, the solution turns red after adding Methyl Red, telling us it's a positive result.

Requirements:

1. Test tube

2. MRVP medium (Glucose phosphate broth)

3. Methyl red indicator

4. Bacterial sample

5. Inoculating loop

Procedure:

1. Take a test tube with MRVP medium.
2. Inoculate it with the bacterial culture using an inoculating loop.
3. Incubate the tube at 37°C for 24 hours.

4. After incubation, add a few drops of Methyl Red indicator to the tube.

Result:

- If the medium turns red → **it shows a positive MR test .(strong acid production).**
- If the medium stays yellow → **it shows a negative MR test.**

Notes:

1. Methyl Red is a pH indicator that changes colour depending on whether the medium is acidic or alkaline.

2. When bacteria produce strong acids by fermentation, the pH drops, and the Methyl Red gives a positive result by turning red.

3. Methyl Red changes colour distinctly at low pH. It turns red if pH is below 4.4.

Voges-Proskauer Test

The Voges-Proskauer (VP) test checks if bacteria can produce neutral end products like acetoin from glucose fermentation.

Principle:

Some bacteria don't produce strong acids; instead, they make a neutral chemical called acetoin when they break down glucose. When we add two special reagents (Barritt's A and B) and shake the tube, if acetoin is there, it reacts with the oxygen and turns red. So a red colour tells us the bacteria made acetoin.

Requirements:

1. Test tube
2. MRVP medium (Glucose phosphate broth)
3. Barritt's reagent A (alpha-naphthol)
4. Barritt's reagent B (KOH)
5. Bacterial sample
6. Inoculating loop

Procedure:

1. Take a test tube with MRVP medium.
2. Inoculate it with the bacterial sample using an inoculating loop.
3. Incubate at 37°C for 24 hours.

4. After incubation, add 10 drops each of Barritt's reagent A and B to the medium.

5. Gently shake the tube to mix and let oxygen from the air get inside.

Result:

- If a red colour appears after 10–30 minutes → **positive VP test (acetoin is produced).**
- If no colour change or a copper colour appears → **negative VP test.**

Notes:

1. VP test detects the presence of acetoin, a neutral substance.

2. Barritt's reagents react with acetoin in the presence of oxygen to give a red colour.

3. A red colour developing within 30 minutes shows a positive VP result.

4. The test needs oxygen for proper colour formation.

Citrate Utilization Test

Principle:

The citrate utilization test is based on the ability of organisms to use citrate as their sole carbon source and ammonium ions as the sole nitrogen source. Organisms that can grow on citrate agar produce an alkaline reaction, leading to a color change in the medium from green to blue due to the pH indicator bromothymol blue.

Requirements:

1. Simmon's citrate agar

2. Bacterial culture

3. Inoculating loop

4. Test tube

Procedure:

1. Take a test tube containing Simmon's citrate agar in slanted form.

2. Inoculate the bacterial culture using a sterilized inoculating loop.

3. Streak it over the slant surface of the agar.

4. Incubate the test tube at 37°C for 24–48 hours.

5. Observe the color of Simmon's citrate agar tube.

Results:

- If the color turns blue, it is positive.
- If the color remains green, it is negative.

Triple Sugar Iron Agar Test

Principle:

The TSI agar test works on the following principles:

1. Sugar fermentation: Bacteria that ferment glucose, lactose, or sucrose produce acid, which turns the medium acidic (yellow).

2. Hydrogen sulfide production: Bacteria that produce hydrogen sulfide (H2S) react with the iron salts, forming a black precipitate of ferrous sulfide.

Composition of TSI Medium:

It is a composite solid agar medium, prepared in a test tube having both a butt and a slant.

The constituents include:

1. Glucose – 0.1%
2. Sucrose – 1%
3. Lactose – 1%
4. Peptone
5. Sodium thiosulfate
6. Ferric salt – H_2S indicator
7. Phenol red – pH indicator
8. NaCl

9. Agar

Procedure:

1. The medium is inoculated with a pure bacterial culture by piercing deep into the butt (stab culture) using a straight wire and then streaking on the slant surface.
2. The tube is then incubated at 37°C for 18–24 hours.

Results:

This test detects three properties of bacteria:

1. Fermentation of sugars to produce acid

2. Gas production

3. H_2S production

- Uninoculated TSI medium is orange-red in color.
- On acid production, it changes to yellow.
- Based on fermentation of sugars in TSI, organisms are categorized into three groups:

1. Non-Fermenters:

i. Do not ferment any sugar.

ii. Alkaline slant and alkaline butt (no change) is observed.

2. Glucose-only Fermenters:

i. Ferment only glucose and produce little acid.

ii. Initially (at \~8 hours), the whole medium turns yellow (acidic).

iii. Later, due to oxidative decarboxylation of peptones, ammonia (NH_3) is produced, making the slant alkaline (red).

iv. This is indicated by a color change slant turns yellow to red due to alkaline byproducts.

Nitrate Reduction Test

Principle:

- Some organisms reduce nitrate (NO_3^-) to nitrite (NO_2^-) or nitrogen gas.
- The nitrites react with sulphanilic acid and N,N-dimethyl-naphthylamine reagent to produce a red color.

Requirements:

1. Peptone water tube
2. Bacterial culture
3. Nitrate disc

Procedure:

1. Put nitrate disc in peptone water tube.
2. Transfer the culture to the tube.
3. Incubate at 37°C for 24 hours.

Results:

Positive : A pink or red color indicates nitrate reduction.

Note:Bacteria convert NO_3^- to NO_2^- by an enzyme called nitrate reductase.

Carbohydrate Fermentation Test

Fermentation is a metabolic process in which some organisms break down substrates such as glucose and sugar under anaerobic conditions into alcohol and gas or organic acids (e.g., lactic acid, formic acid, acetic acid, butyric acid).

Principle:

- The medium used in this test is a nutrient broth that contains fermentable carbohydrate (glucose, lactose, sucrose, mannitol, etc.) and a pH indicator, phenol red.

- Phenol red is red at neutral pH and turns *yellow* at pH below 6.8 due to production of organic acids.

Note:The color change only occurs when sufficient amount of acid is produced by the bacteria.

- To detect gas formation, a Durham tube is used. This is a small tube placed in an inverted position in the fermentation tube.

Requirements:

1. Bacterial culture

2. Nutrient broth

3. Durham tube

Procedure:

1. Preparation of fermentation medium:

- Peptone – 10 g
- Carbohydrate – 5 g
- Sodium chloride – 15 g
- Phenol red – 0.018 g
- Distilled water – 1000 ml
- pH – 7.3

2. Broth is taken into the fermentation tube and insert Durham's tube in it and screw-cap the tube.
3. Autoclave the tube at 15 psi pressure for 15 mins at 121°C.
4. Inoculate the specific fermentation tube with the organism provided.
5. Incubate the fermentation tube at 37°C for 24–48 hrs.
6. Examine the tube for acid and gas production.

Result:

- ***Positive test:***

1. ***Acid production: medium turns yellow.***
2. ***Acid & gas production: medium turns yellow with gas in Durham's tube.***

Oxidation Fermentation Test

This test is done to differentiate between oxidative bacteria and fermentative bacteria.

Note:Bacteria that produce acid from carbohydrates under aerobic conditions only are called oxidative.Developed by Hugh and Leifson.

Hugh Leifson Medium:

- Peptone amount is low.
- The medium is semisolid in consistency – it facilitates the motility of organisms.
- Peptone concentration is decreased to minimize the formation of alkaline products.
- Carbohydrate concentration is increased to enhance the production of acid.

Principle:

The bromothymol blue turns green to yellow in acidic concentration.This test is used to determine if a gram-negative organism metabolizes carbohydrate oxidatively, by fermentation, or is non-saccharolytic (shows no ability to use the carbohydrate in the medium).

Requirements:

1. Two test tubes

2. Hugh and Leifson medium

3. Bacterial culture

Procedure:

- Take two test tubes containing Hugh and Leifson medium.

Note:You have to perform the experiment with both test tubes in different conditions, i.e.,

1. Tube-1 (Aerobically) → in presence of air
2. Tube-2 (Anaerobically) → in absence of air

- ***In test tube 1:***

1. Add the bacterial culture with the help of an inoculating wire in the manner of stab culture.
2. If the color of the medium changes from green to yellow, it means the bacteria is oxidative.

- ***In test tube 2:***

1. Add the bacterial culture with the help of an inoculating wire in the manner of stab culture.
2. Seal the opening of the tube with paraffin wax to block the supply of air or to create an anaerobic environment.
3. If the medium changes from green to red, it means the bacteria is fermentative.

NOTE: The color change is due to the formation of acidic conditions.

Hydrogen Sulfide production Test

Note:H_2S is produced by bacteria when they metabolize sulfur-containing compounds and proteins during bacterial enzyme activity.

Principle:

A medium with iron salts and a sulfur-containing compound is inoculated with the test organism and incubated.

If H_2S is produced, it combines with iron salts to form ferric sulfide (FeS) in the tube that results in a positive reaction.

Test Methods:

1. Triple Sugar Iron Agar

2. Sulfite Agar – Selective medium for producing H_2S bacteria.

3. Lead Acetate Paper– A simple, rapid test using lead acetate-impregnated paper.

Procedure

➢ ***Triple Sugar Iron Agar Method:***

1. Prepare TSI Agar plate.

2. With the help of sterilized inoculating needle, stab-inoculate the bacteria into TSI Agar slant.

3. Incubate the tube at 37°C for 24 hours.

4. Examine the tube for color change.

➢ ***Sulfite Agar Method:***

1. Prepare sulfite agar plate.

2. With the help of inoculation loop, streak the test bacterium onto the surface of the agar plate.

3. Incubate the plate at 37°C for 24 hours.

4. Examine the plate for color change.

➢ ***Lead Acetate Paper Method:***

1. Cut lead acetate papers into strips and moisten with distilled water.

2. Place a small amount of test bacterium on the paper.

3. Seal the paper in a container and incubate at 37°C for 24 hours.

4. Examine the paper for color change.

Results:

- **H_2S Positive:**Blackening or darkening of medium/paper.
- **H_2S Negative:**No color change / Slight yellowing.

CAMP Test

CAMP:

C – Christie

A – Atkins

M – Munch

P – Peterson

It is a test used for differentiating Streptococcus agalactiae (Group-B) [CAMP Positive] from other Streptococci spp.

Principle:

The CAMP test checks for a special reaction between two types of bacteria:

1. Group B Streptococcus (the bacteria being tested)

2. Staphylococcus aureus (a known bacteria)

When these two bacteria are near each other, they work together to break down red blood cells (a process called hemolysis). This creates a clear area (like an arrowhead shape) where the red blood cells are broken down.

Procedure:

1. Take a petri dish containing blood agar.
2. Streak a straight line of Streptococcus agalactiae at the center of the petri dish.

3. Streak a perpendicular line on the right side of Staphylococcus aureus.

4. Incubate the petri dish at 37°C for 24 hours.

5. Observe the hemolysis on the line of Staphylococcus aureus.

Results:

If an arrow-shaped hemolysis is observed around Streptococcus agalactiae, it indicates CAMP positive.

Nagler's Reaction

- *It is used to differentiate between Clostridium perfringens from other spp. species.*
- *Clostridium perfringens produces α-toxin that contains lecithinase enzyme, which is a kind of phospholipase.*

Principle:

The α-toxin or the lecithinase enzyme converts the lecithin (present in media containing egg yolk) into diglycerides that get deposited around the bacterial colonies.

Requirements:

1. Media containing egg yolk

2. Anti α-toxin

3. Bacterial colony

Procedure:

1. Take a petri dish containing egg yolk medium.

2. Mark a line on the petri dish dividing it into two halves with the help of a marker.

3. Add anti α-toxin to one side.

4.Streak the organism on both halves with the help of an inoculating loop.

5. Incubate the petri dish at 37°C for 24-48 hours.

Results:

Positive result is opacity around the colonies.

Hippurate Hydrolysis Test

PRINCIPLE:

This test is based on the ability of bacteria (Streptococcus agalactiae) to hydrolyze hippurate to glycine and benzoic acid by the action of an enzyme, hippuricase.Hippuricase → Glycine + Benzoic acid

It also involves ninhydrin, the reduction of ninhydrin by the oxidizing action of glycine, resulting in a purple-colored complex.Glycine + Ninhydrin → Purple-colored complex

REAGENTS:

1. Hippurate solution
2. Ninhydrin solution
3. Test tubes
4. Distilled water
5. Inoculating loop

PROCEDURE:

1. Take a test tube half-filled with hippurate solution.

2. Add two colonies of organism from the culture to the test tube with the help of an inoculating loop.

3. Incubate the test tube for 2 hours at 37°C.

4. After two hours of incubation, add two drops of ninhydrin to the test tube.

5. Reincubate the tube at 37°C for 30 minutes.

6. Observe the test tube at an interval of 10-15 minutes of time.

RESULT:

- **POSITIVE:** Hippurate hydrolysis is indicated by a deep blue color.
- **NEGATIVE:** Result indicates no faint purple color or no color change.

CONTROL ORGANISM:

Streptococcus agalactiae → Hippurate +ve

Streptococcus pyogenes → Hippurate -ve

NOTE: The colony should be picked carefully as not to pick agar, which contains protein.

Bile Solubility Test

It is a test used to differentiate or confirm Streptococcus pneumoniae from other alpha-hemolytic streptococci.It is an essential test for distinguishing between S. pneumoniae and Streptococcus pseudopneumoniae.

NOTE:The exact mechanism of the test is not clearly understood, but it is hypothesized that lysis occurs due to the induction of autolytic enzymes.

Principle:

The test is based on the lysis of pneumococcal cells when sodium deoxycholate (bile salt) is applied under specific conditions, while other streptococci do not lyse.

S. pneumoniae possesses an intracellular autolytic enzyme, an amidase that causes the organism to undergo rapid autolysis when grown on an artificial medium.The bile salts alter the surface tension and cause cell membrane rearrangement.

Requirements:

1. 2% Sodium deoxycholate solution: Dissolve 2 grams of bile salt into 100 mL sterile distilled water.

2. 10% Sodium deoxycholate solution: Dissolve 10 grams of bile salt into 100 mL sterile distilled water.

3. 0.85% NaCl solution

Procedure:

1. Prepare a heavy suspension of a pure culture in 2 mL of 0.85% saline.

2. Divide the organism suspension into two tubes.

3. Adjust the turbidity to the level of 0.5 McFarland standard.

4. To one tube, add 2 drops of 2% bile salt solution and mix.

5. To the other tube, add 2 drops of sterile distilled water and mix.

6. Leave both tubes for 10–15 minutes at 37°C.

7. Observe for a clearing of turbidity in the tube containing 2% bile salt.

8. If negative, continue to incubate for up to 2 hours and observe again.

Results:

- **Positive Result:** Clearing of turbidity in the tube containing 2% bile salt solution, indicating lysis of S. pneumoniae cells.
- **Negative Result:** No clearing of turbidity in the tube containing 2% bile salt solution, suggesting the presence of other streptococcal species

Bibliography

1. Collee, J. G., Fraser, A. G., Marmion, B. P., & Simmons, A. (1996). *Mackie & McCartney Practical Medical Microbiology* (14th ed.). New York: Churchill Livingstone.

2. Ananthanarayan, R., & Paniker, C. K. J. (2024). *Ananthanarayan and Paniker's Textbook of Microbiology* (13th ed.). Hyderabad: Universities Press (India) Pvt. Ltd.

3. Singh, B., & Singh, R. (2020). *Microbiology for Medical Sciences* (1st ed.). New Delhi: Dreamtech Press.

4. Cappuccino, J. G., & Welsh, C. (2019). *Microbiology: A Laboratory Manual* (11th ed.). Boston: Pearson.

5. Forbes, B. A., Sahm, D. F., & Weissfeld, A. S. (2007). *Bailey & Scott's Diagnostic Microbiology* (12th ed.). St. Louis: Mosby Elsevier.

6. Tille, P. (2016). *Bailey & Scott's Diagnostic Microbiology* (14th ed.). St. Louis: Elsevier Health Sciences.